HAL•LEONARD

ESSENTIAL SONGS

PIANO VOCAL GUITAR

Broadway

ISBN 0-634-09841-1

HAL•LEONARD® CORPORATION

7777 W. BLUEMOUND RD. P.O. BOX 13819 MILWAUKEE, WI 53213

Visit Hal Leonard Online at
www.halleonard.com

CONTENTS

AND ALL THAT JAZZ
from CHICAGO

Words by FRED EBB
Music by JOHN KANDER

her where to park her gir-dle, Oh, _____ her moth-er's blood-'d cur-dle if she'd hear _ her

ba-by's queer _ for all that jazz! _____

_ Find a flask, _ we're play-ing fast and loose _ and all that jazz! _

Oh, _____ you're gon-na see your She-ba shim-my shake, _ and

all that jazz! _ Oh, _____ I'm gon-na shim-my till my gar-ters break, _ and

Right up here _ is where I store the juice, _ and all that jazz! _

ANY DREAM WILL DO

from JOSEPH AND THE AMAZING TECHNICOLOR® DREAMCOAT

Music by ANDREW LLOYD WEBBER
Lyrics by TIM RICE

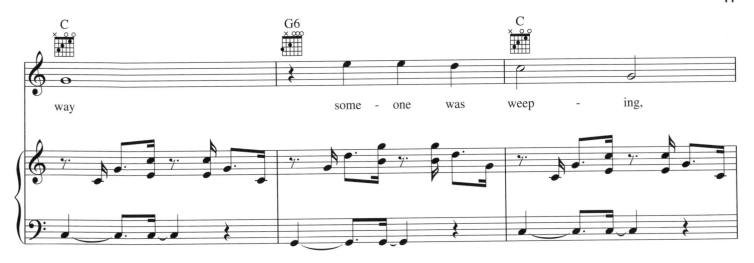

way   some - one was weep - ing,

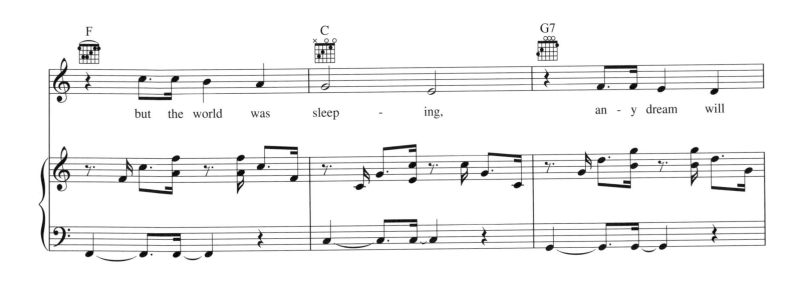

but the world was sleep - ing,   an - y dream will

do.   I wore my coat

CHOIR:

I wore my

APPLAUSE
from the Broadway Musical APPLAUSE

Lyric by LEE ADAMS
Music by CHARLES STROUSE

AS IF WE NEVER SAID GOODBYE

from SUNSET BOULEVARD

Music by ANDREW LLOYD WEBBER
Lyrics by DON BLACK and CHRISTOPHER HAMPTON,
with contributions by AMY POWERS

NORMA: I don't know why I'm fright - ened __ I know my way a - round here. __ The card - board trees, the paint - ed seas, __ the sound here. __ Yes, a world to re - dis - cov - er, __

THE BEST OF TIMES

from LA CAGE AUX FOLLES

Music and Lyric by
JERRY HERMAN

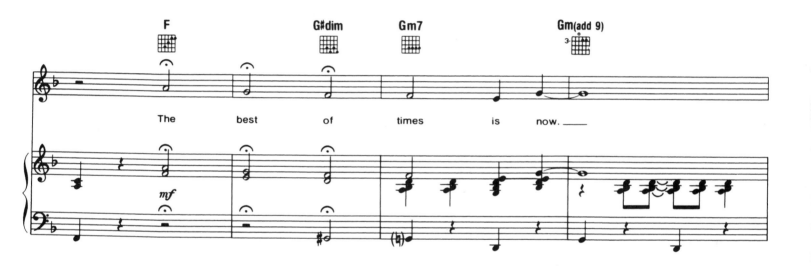

The best of times is now. _____

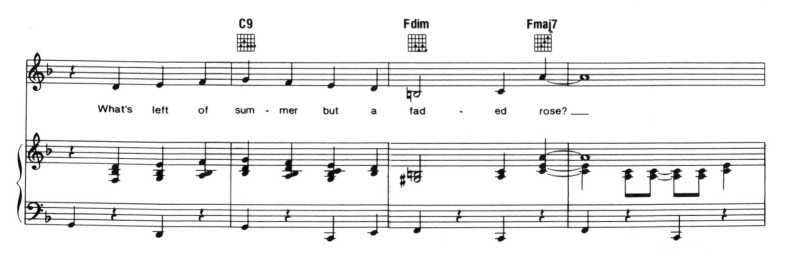

What's left of sum - mer but a fad - ed rose? _____

BEAUTY AND THE BEAST

from Walt Disney's BEAUTY AND THE BEAST: THE BROADWAY MUSICAL

Lyrics by HOWARD ASHMAN
Music by ALAN MENKEN

BEWITCHED
from PAL JOEY

Words by LORENZ HART
Music by RICHARD RODGERS

Moderately

Not fast

He's a fool and don't I know it, But a fool can have his charms;

I'm in love and don't I show it, Like a babe in arms.

Love's the same old sad sen-sa-tion, Late-ly I've not slept a wink,

BIG D
from THE MOST HAPPY FELLA

By FRANK LOESSER

CAN'T HELP LOVIN' DAT MAN

from SHOW BOAT

Lyrics by OSCAR HAMMERSTEIN II
Music by JEROME KERN

Slowly

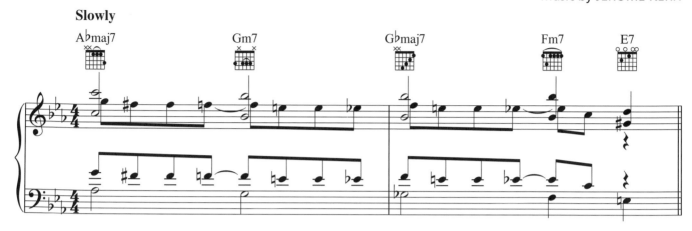

Fish got to swim___ and birds got to fly,___ I got to love___ one
Tell me he's la - zy, tell me he's slow,___ tell me I'm cra - zy,

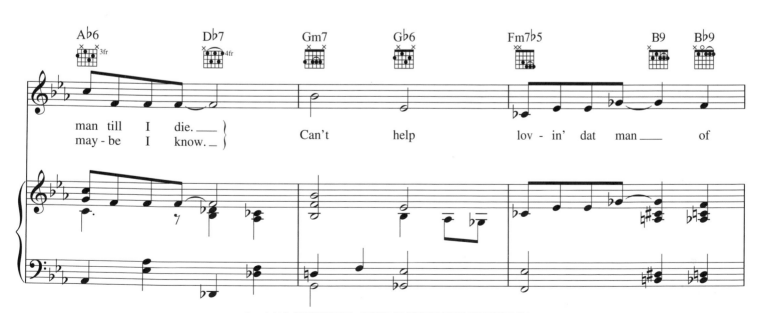

man till I die.___ }
may - be I know.___ } Can't help lov - in' dat man ___ of

BLUE SKIES
from BETSY

Words and Music by
IRVING BERLIN

A BUSHEL AND A PECK
from GUYS AND DOLLS

By FRANK LOESSER

CABARET
from the Musical CABARET

Words by FRED EBB
Music by JOHN KANDER

CIRCLE OF LIFE

Disney Presents THE LION KING: THE BROADWAY MUSICAL

Music by ELTON JOHN
Lyrics by TIM RICE

COME RAIN OR COME SHINE
from ST. LOUIS WOMAN

Words by JOHNNY MERCER
Music by HAROLD ARLEN

DANCING QUEEN

from MAMMA MIA!

Words and Music by BENNY ANDERSSON,
BJORN ULVAEUS and STIG ANDERSON

Strong Rock

You can dance. You can jive, having the time of your life. Oh, see that girl.

DAY BY DAY
from the Musical GODSPELL

Words and Music by
STEPHEN SCHWARTZ

DO I HEAR A WALTZ?

from DO I HEAR A WALTZ?

Music by RICHARD RODGERS
Lyrics by STEPHEN SONDHEIM

Tempo di Valse Allegro

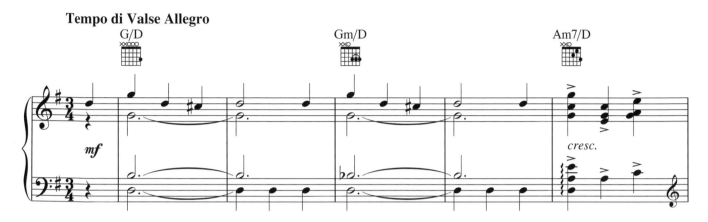

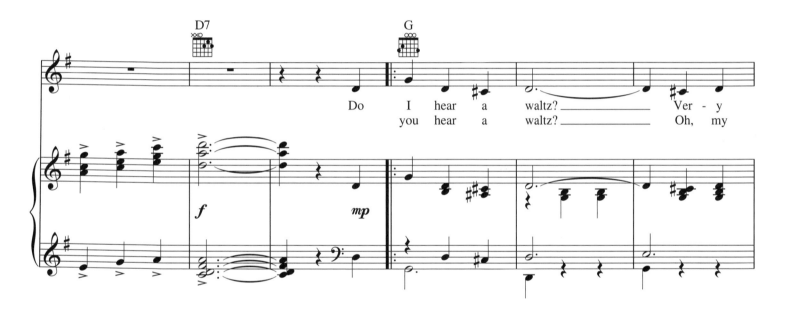

Do I hear a waltz? _____ Ver - y
you hear a waltz? _____ Oh, my

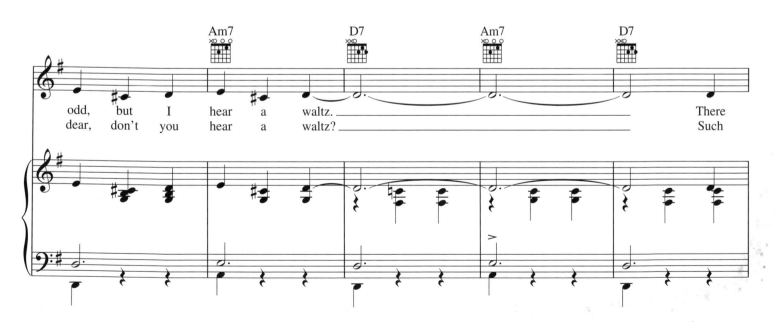

odd, but I hear a waltz. _____ There
dear, don't you hear a waltz? _____ Such

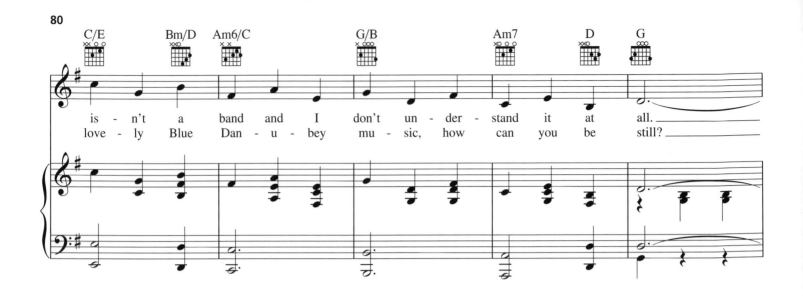

is - n't a band and I don't un - der - stand it at all. ____
love - ly Blue Dan - u - bey mu - sic, how can you be still? ____

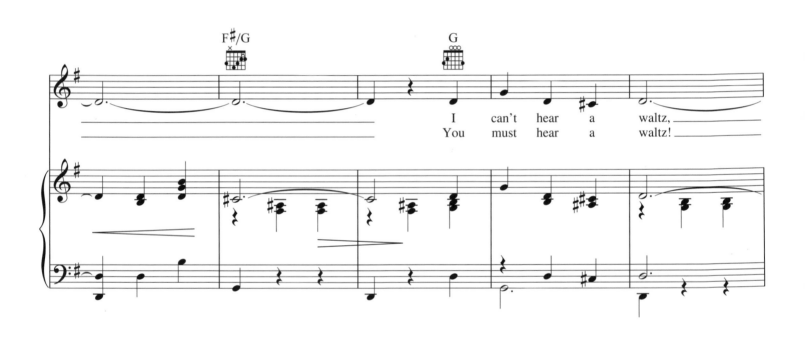

I can't hear a waltz, ____
You must hear a waltz! ____

__ Oh, my Lord, there it goes a - gain! ____ Why is
__ E - ven strang - ers are danc - ing now: ____ An old

DO I LOVE YOU BECAUSE YOU'RE BEAUTIFUL?

from CINDERELLA

Lyrics by OSCAR HAMMERSTEIN II
Music by RICHARD RODGERS

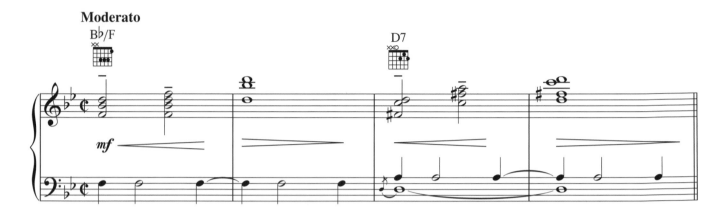

Do I love you be-cause you're beau-ti-ful? _____ Or are you beau - ti - ful _____ be - cause I love you? _____

EDELWEISS
from THE SOUND OF MUSIC

Lyrics by OSCAR HAMMERSTEIN II
Music by RICHARD RODGERS

DON'T CRY FOR ME ARGENTINA
from EVITA

Words by TIM RICE
Music by ANDREW LLOYD WEBBER

DON'T CRY OUT LOUD
(We Don't Cry Out Loud)
from THE BOY FROM OZ

Words and Music by PETER ALLEN
and CAROLE BAYER SAGER

Don't cry __ out loud, _____ just keep it in - side, learn how to
Fly high __ and proud, _____ and if you should fall re - mem - ber you

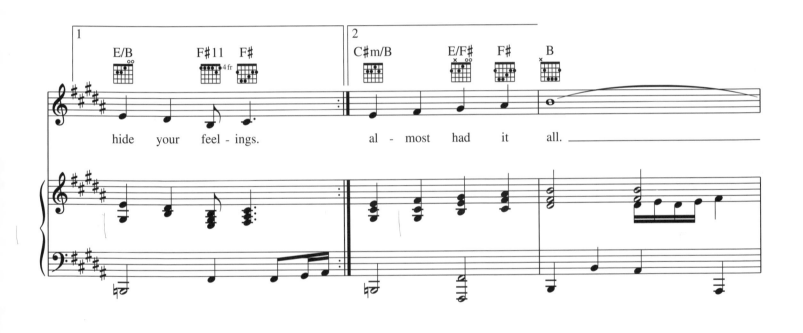

hide your feel - ings. al - most had it all. _____

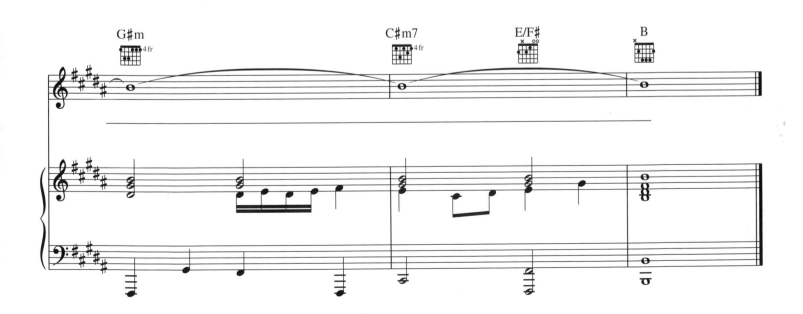

EASTER PARADE
from AS THOUSANDS CHEER

Words and Music by
IRVING BERLIN

Nev-er saw you look quite so pret-ty be - fore. ___

Nev-er saw you dressed quite so love-ly, what's more ___

EV'RY TIME WE SAY GOODBYE

from SEVEN LIVELY ARTS

Words and Music by
COLE PORTER

FALLING IN LOVE WITH LOVE
from THE BOYS FROM SYRACUSE

Words by LORENZ HART
Music by RICHARD RODGERS

112

FOLLOW YOUR HEART

from URINETOWN

Music and Lyrics by MARK HOLLMANN
Book and Lyrics by GREG KOTIS

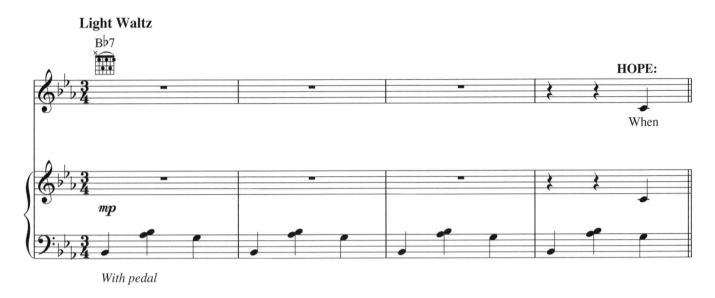

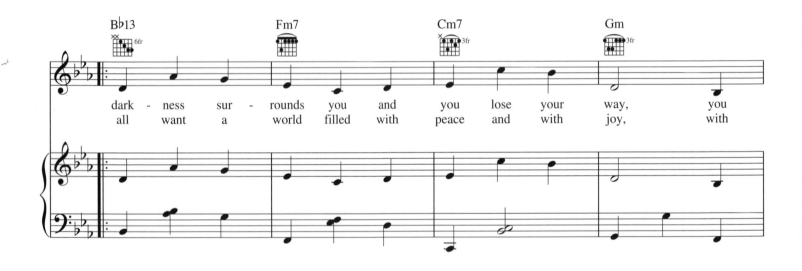

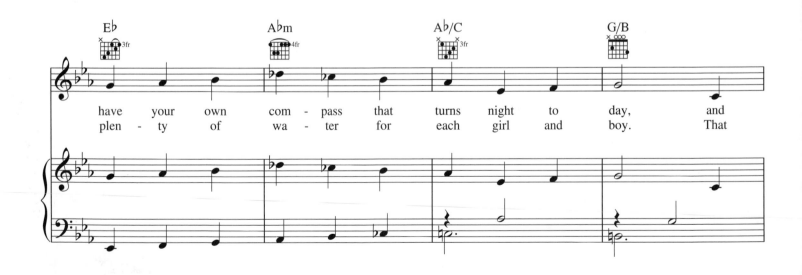

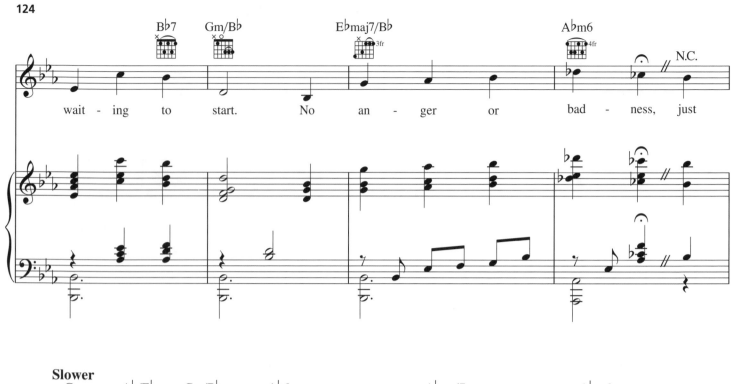

waiting to start. No anger or badness, just

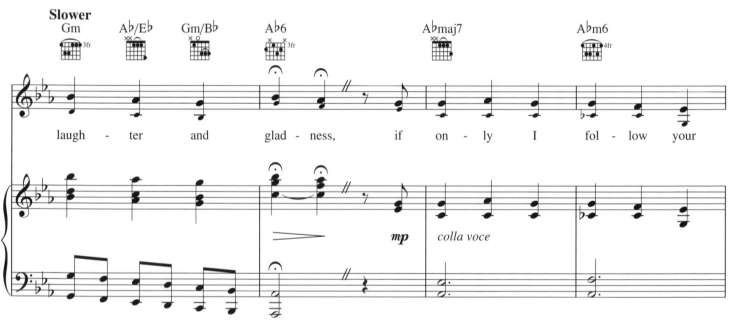

Slower

laughter and gladness, if only I follow your

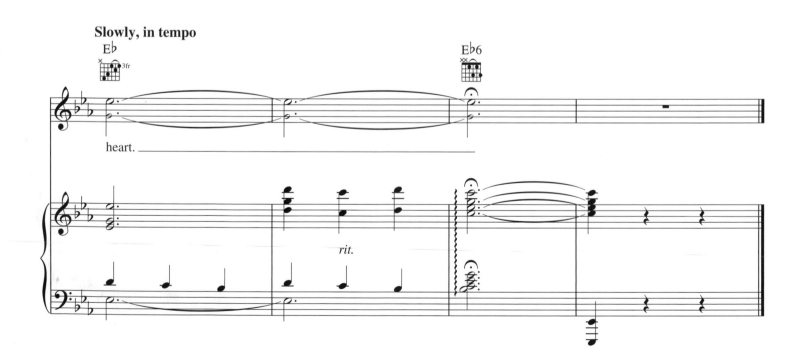

Slowly, in tempo

heart.

HELLO, DOLLY!
from HELLO, DOLLY!

Music and Lyric by
JERRY HERMAN

FRIENDSHIP
from DUBARRY WAS A LADY

Words and Music by
COLE PORTER

GLAD TO BE UNHAPPY

from ON YOUR TOES

Words by LORENZ HART
Music by RICHARD RODGERS

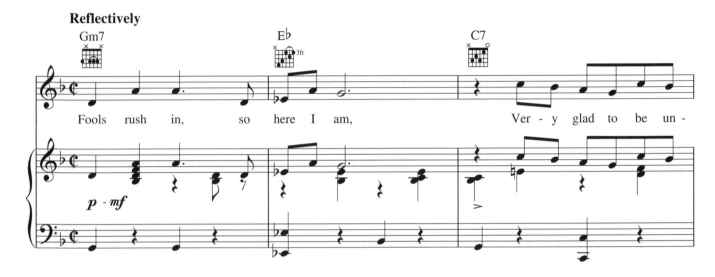

Fools rush in, so here I am, Ver-y glad to be un-

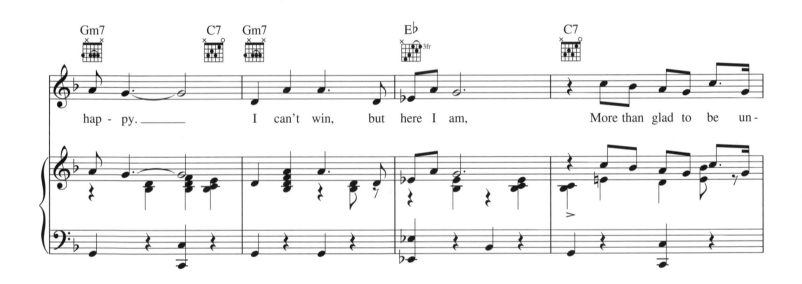

hap-py. _____ I can't win, but here I am, More than glad to be un-

hap-py. _____ Un-re-quit-ed love's a bore, And I've got it pret-ty

HARD CANDY CHRISTMAS

from THE BEST LITTLE WHOREHOUSE IN TEXAS

Words and Music by
CAROL HALL

HOW TO HANDLE A WOMAN

from CAMELOT

Words by ALAN JAY LERNER
Music by FREDERICK LOEWE

I CAN'T GET STARTED WITH YOU

from ZIEGFELD FOLLIES

Words by IRA GERSHWIN
Music by VERNON DUKE

I'm a glum one,
it's ex-plain-a-ble: I met some-one un-at-tain-a-ble.
Life's a bore, the world is my oy-ster no

I DON'T KNOW HOW TO LOVE HIM

from JESUS CHRIST SUPERSTAR

Words by TIM RICE
Music by ANDREW LLOYD WEBBER

I ENJOY BEING A GIRL
from FLOWER DRUM SONG

Lyrics by OSCAR HAMMERSTEIN II
Music by RICHARD RODGERS

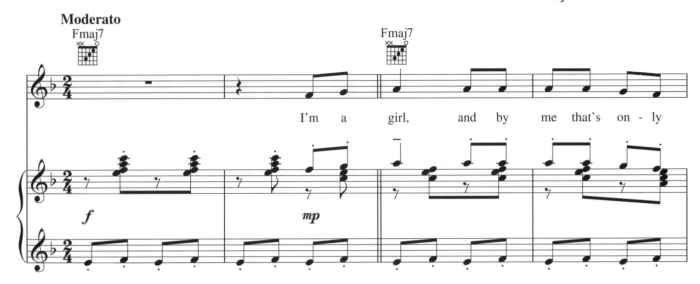

I LOVE PARIS

from CAN-CAN

Words and Music by
COLE PORTER

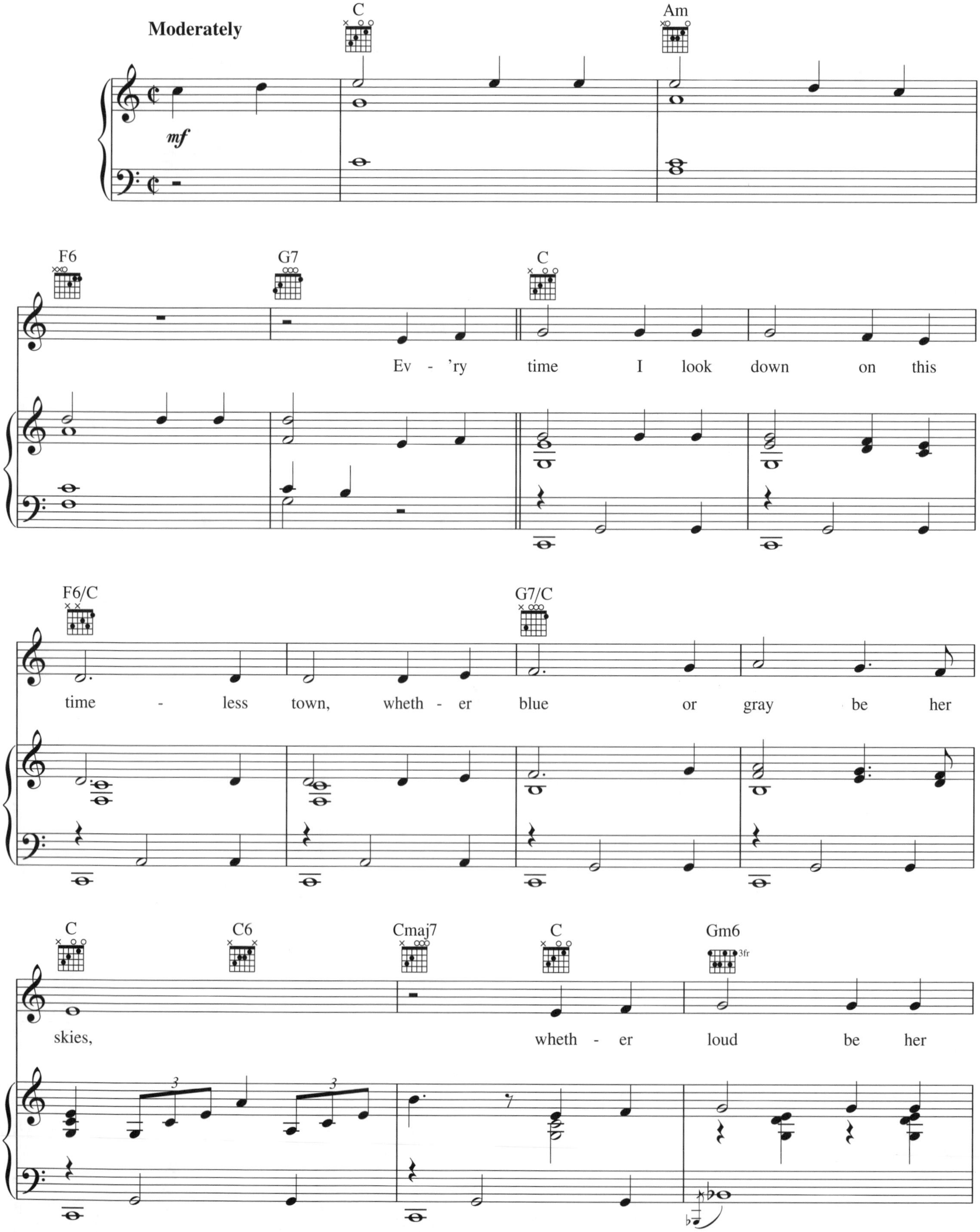

Moderately
C
Am
mf
F6
G7
C
Ev - 'ry time I look down on this
F6/C
G7/C
time - less town, wheth - er blue or gray be her
C
C6
Cmaj7
C
Gm6
3fr
skies, wheth - er loud be her

cheers, or wheth - er soft be her tears, more and more

do I re - al - ize:

Slow Fox Trot

I love Par - is in the spring - time, _____

I love Par - is in the fall, _____

I LOVE YOU

from MEXICAN HAYRIDE

Words and Music by
COLE PORTER

I'LL BE SEEING YOU

from RIGHT THIS WAY

Lyric by IRVING KAHAL
Music by SAMMY FAIN

Moderately

Ca - the-dral bells were toll - ing _____ And our hearts sang on, _____ Was it the spell of Par - is _____ Or the A - pril dawn? _____ Who knows, _____ if we shall meet a - gain?

I'M GONNA WASH THAT MAN RIGHT OUTA MY HAIR

Lyrics by OSCAR HAMMERSTEIN II
Music by RICHARD RODGERS

I'VE GROWN ACCUSTOMED TO HER FACE

from MY FAIR LADY

Words by ALAN JAY LERNER
Music by FREDERICK LOEWE

IF HE WALKED INTO MY LIFE

from MAME

Music and Lyric by
JERRY HERMAN

IF I RULED THE WORLD

from PICKWICK

Words by LESLIE BRICUSSE
Music by CYRIL ORNADEL

Steady, moderate tempo

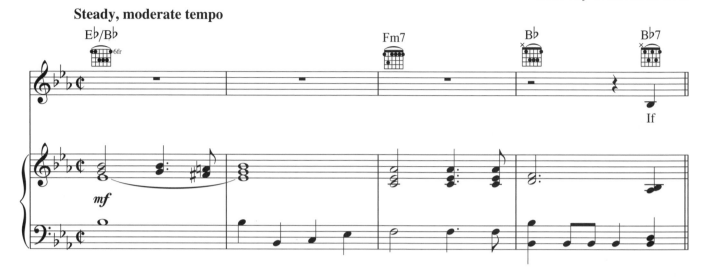

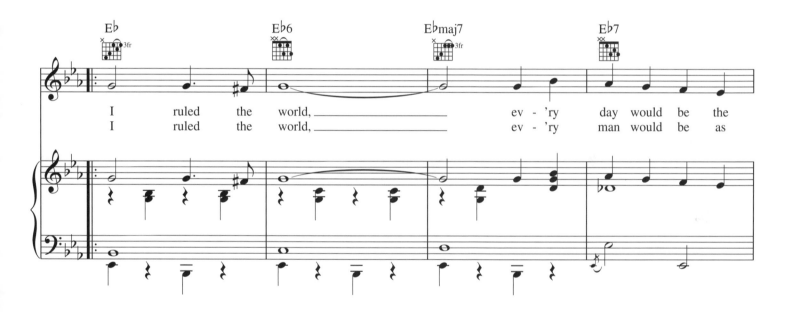

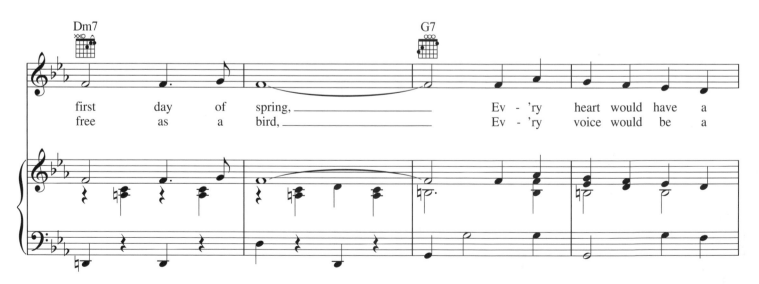

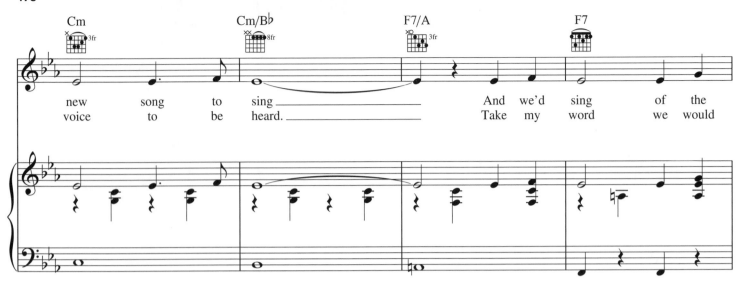

new song to sing _____ And we'd sing of the
voice to to be heard. _____ Take my word of we would

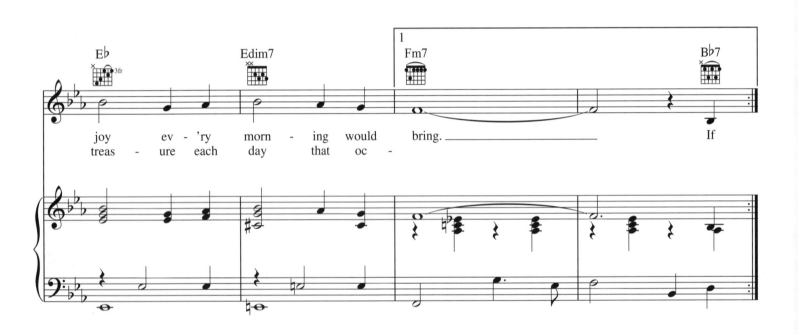

joy ev - 'ry morn - ing would bring. _____ If
treas - ure each day that oc -

curred. _____ My world _____ would be a

THE IMPOSSIBLE DREAM
(The Quest)
from MAN OF LA MANCHA

Lyric by JOE DARION
Music by MITCH LEIGH

IT MIGHT AS WELL BE SPRING

from STATE FAIR

Lyrics by OSCAR HAMMERSTEIN II
Music by RICHARD RODGERS

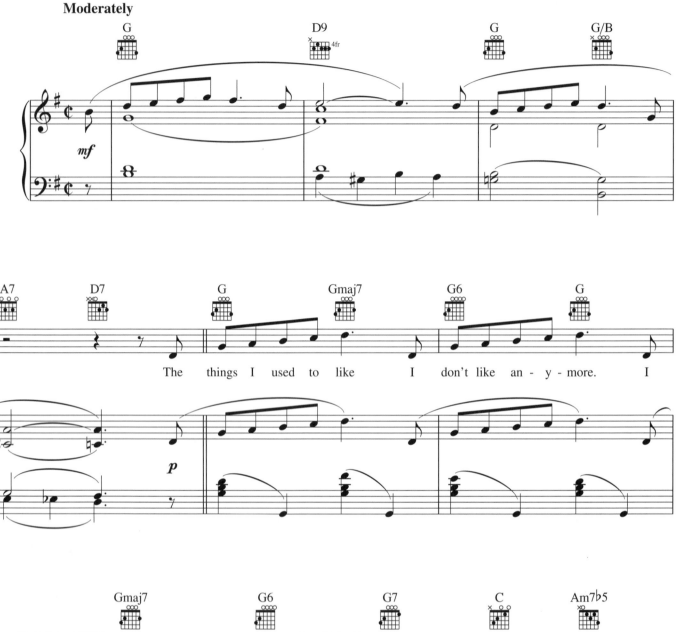

The things I used to like I don't like an-y-more. I want a lot of oth-er things I've nev-er had be-fore. It's just like moth-er

IT'S A LOVELY DAY TODAY

from the Stage Production CALL ME MADAM

Words and Music by
IRVING BERLIN

It's a love-ly day to-day. ___ So what-ev-er you've got to do, ___ you've got a love-ly day to do it in, ___ that's true. ___ And I

JUNE IS BUSTIN' OUT ALL OVER

from CAROUSEL

Lyrics by OSCAR HAMMERSTEIN II
Music by RICHARD RODGERS

hug - gin' the be - jeeb - ers Out - a all the morn - in' glo - ries on the
cause the Cap - tains hank - er Fer a com - fort they ken on - ly get in
ter - mined there'll be new sheep And the ewe sheep are - n't e - ven keep - in'

fence! _____ Be - cause it's June! _____ June, June,
port! _____ Be - cause it's June! _____ June, June,
score! _____ On a - count - a it's June! _____ June, June,

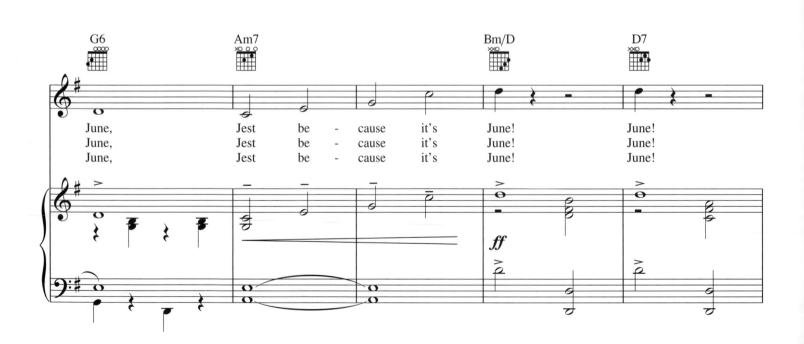

June, Jest be - cause it's June! June!
June, Jest be - cause it's June! June!
June, Jest be - cause it's June! June!

KIDS!
from BYE BYE BIRDIE

Lyric by LEE ADAMS
Music by CHARLES STROUSE

LOOK FOR THE SILVER LINING

from SALLY

Words by BUDDY DeSYLVA
Music by JEROME KERN

LITTLE GIRL BLUE
from JUMBO

Words by LORENZ HART
Music by RICHARD RODGERS

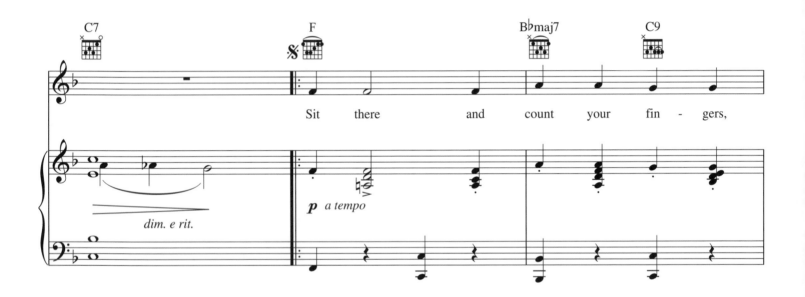

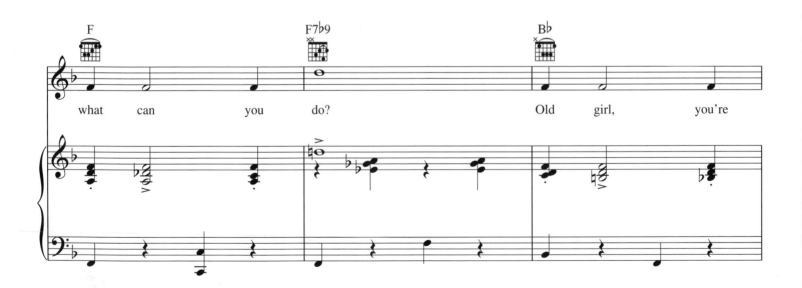

LOVE CHANGES EVERYTHING

from ASPECTS OF LOVE

Music by ANDREW LLOYD WEBBER
Lyrics by DON BLACK and CHARLES HART

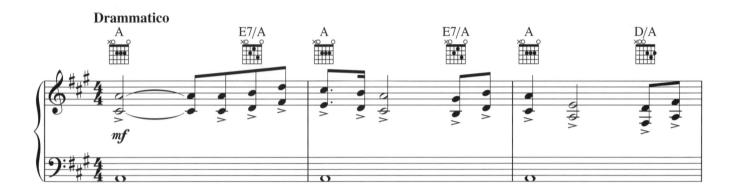

Love,   love chang - es ev - 'ry - thing: hands and
Love,   love chang - es ev - 'ry - thing: days are

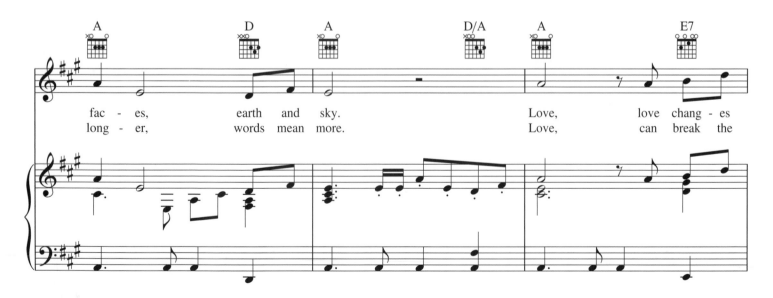

fac - es,   earth and sky.   Love,   love chang - es
long - er,   words mean more.   Love,   can break the

ev - 'ry - thing: how you live and how you die.
strong - est heart, pain is deep - er than be - fore.

Love _____ can make the sum - mer fly or a night seem like a
Love _____ will turn your world a - round and that world will last for -

life - time. Yes love, _____ love chang - es ev - 'ry - thing: now I
ev - er. Yes love, _____ love chang - es ev - 'ry - thing; brings you

trem - ble at your name. Noth - ing in the world will ev - er
glo - ry, brings you shame. Noth - ing in the world will ev - er

cresc.

MEMORY
from CATS

Music by ANDREW LLOYD WEBBER
Text by TREVOR NUNN after T.S. ELIOT

GRIZABELLA:

Mid - night. _____ Not a sound from the pave - ment. _____ Has the moon lost her

Mem - ory _____ all a - lone in the moon - light _____ I can smile at the

mem - ory? _____ She is smil-ing a - lone. _____ In the

old days, _____ I was beau - ti - ful then. _____ I re -

Burnt out ends of smo- ky days, ___ the stale cold smell ___ of

sun. _____ If you touch me you'll un - der - stand what

hap - pi - ness is. Look a new day has be -

gun.

MANHATTAN

from the Broadway Musical THE GARRICK GAIETIES

Words by LORENZ HART
Music by RICHARD RODGERS

We'll set - tle down right here in town.

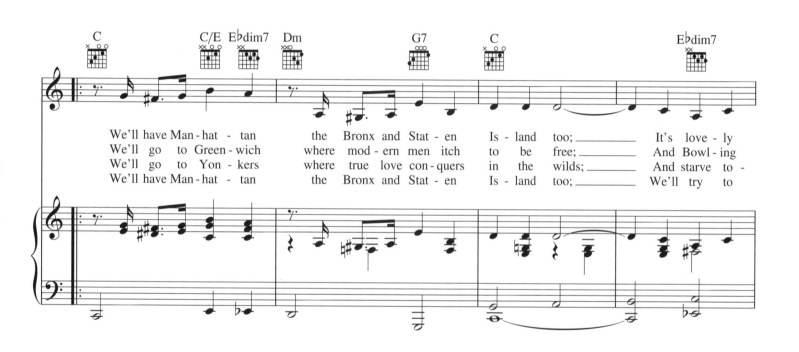

We'll have Man - hat - tan the Bronx and Stat - en Is - land too; _____ It's love - ly
We'll go to Green - wich where mod - ern men itch to be free; _____ And Bowl - ing
We'll go to Yon - kers where true love con - quers in the wilds; _____ And starve to -
We'll have Man - hat - tan the Bronx and Stat - en Is - land too; _____ We'll try to

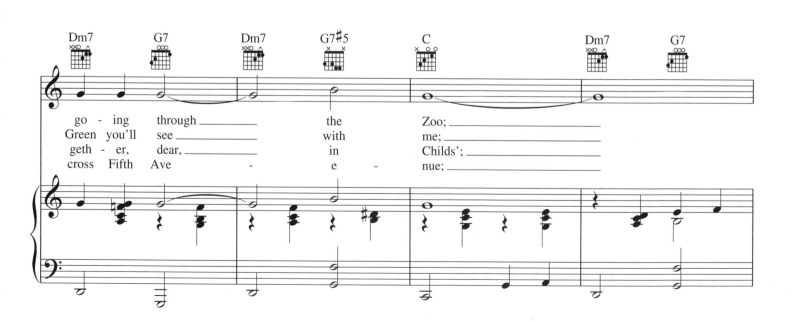

go - ing through _____ the Zoo; _____
Green you'll see _____ with me; _____
geth - er, dear, in Childs'; _____
cross Fifth Ave - e - nue; _____

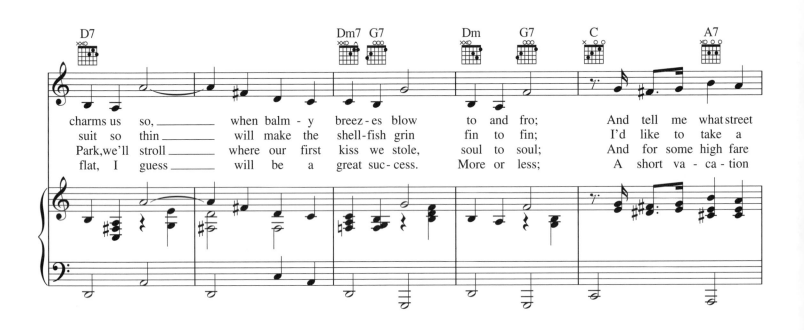

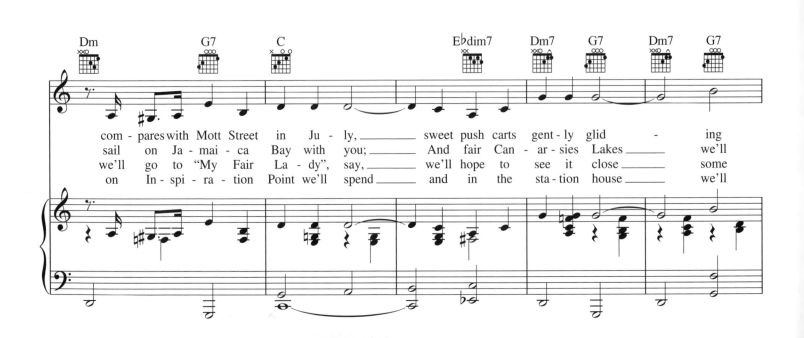

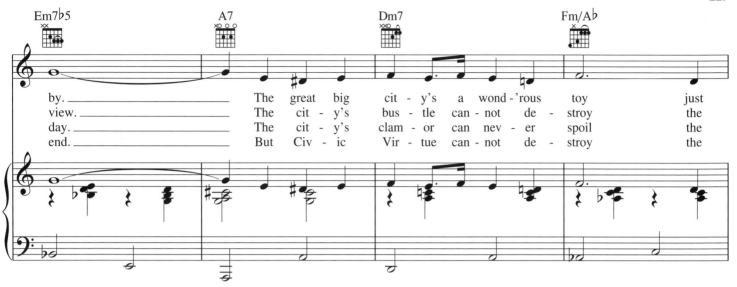

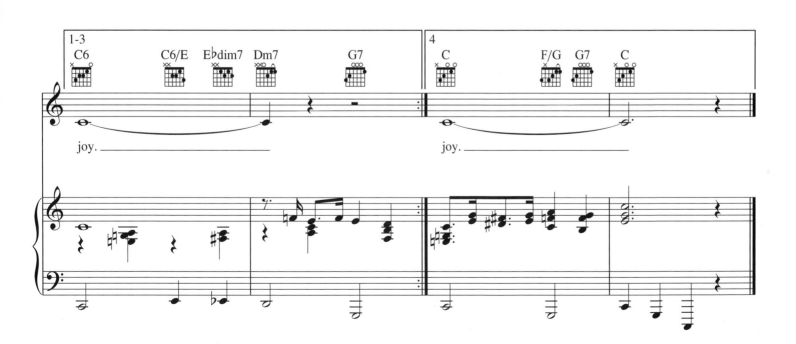

MOOD INDIGO
from SOPHISTICATED LADIES

Words and Music by DUKE ELLINGTON,
IRVING MILLS and ALBANY BIGARD

THE MUSIC OF THE NIGHT
from THE PHANTOM OF THE OPERA

Music by ANDREW LLOYD WEBBER
Lyrics by CHARLES HART
Additional Lyrics by RICHARD STILGOE

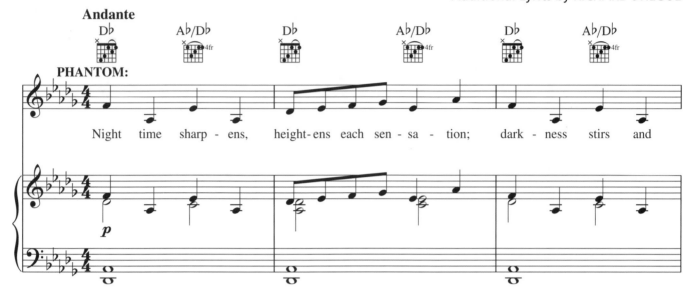

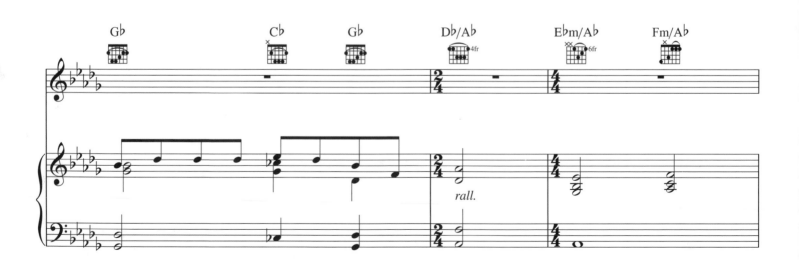

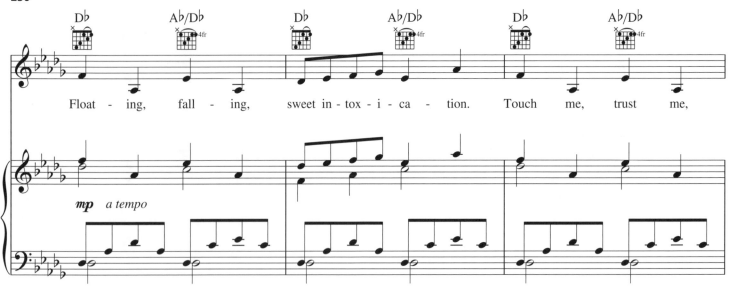

Float - ing, fall - ing, sweet in - tox - i - ca - tion. Touch me, trust me,

sa - vour each sen - sa - tion. Let the dream be - gin, let your dark - er side give in to the

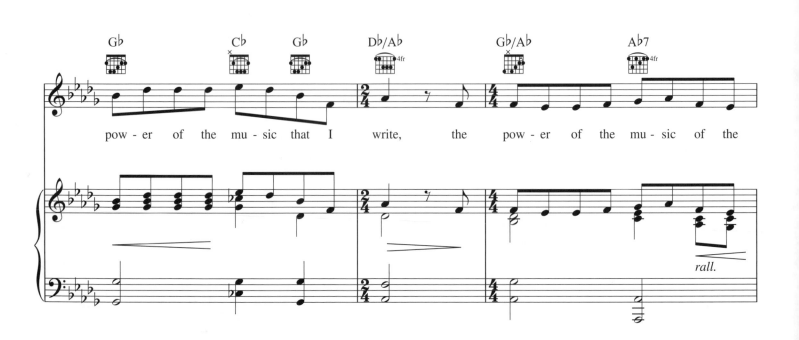

pow - er of the mu - sic that I write, the pow - er of the mu - sic of the

MY CUP RUNNETH OVER

from I DO! I DO!

Words by TOM JONES
Music by HARVEY SCHMIDT

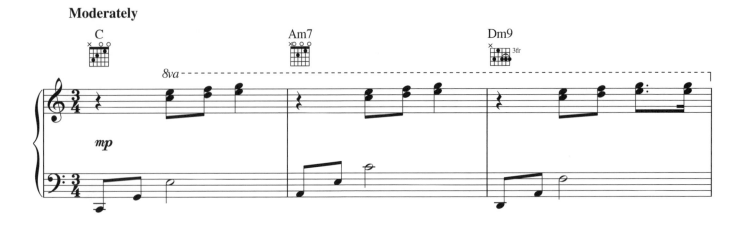

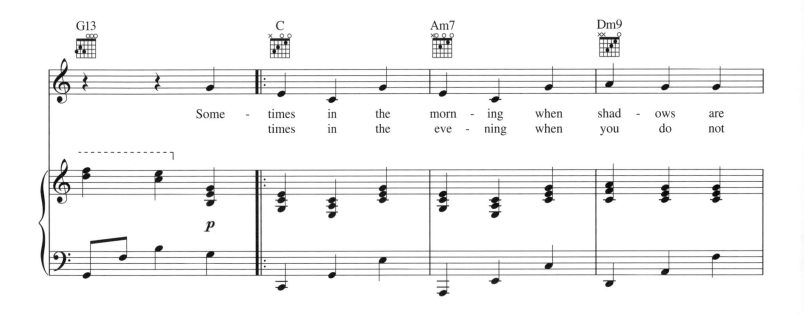

Some - times in the morn - ing when shad - ows are
times in the eve - ning when when you do not

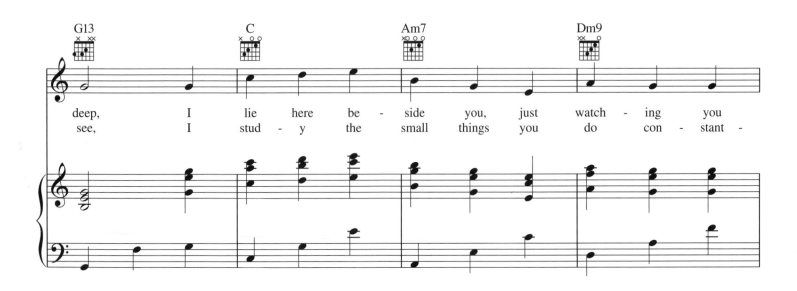

deep, I lie here be - side you, just watch - ing you
see, I stud - y the small things you do con - stant -

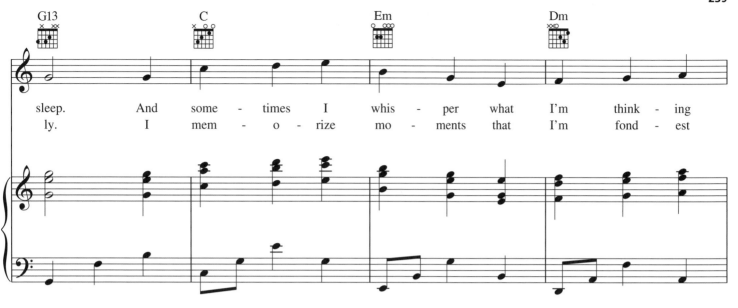

sleep. And some - times I whis - per what I'm think - ing
ly. I mem - o - rize mo - ments that I'm fond - est

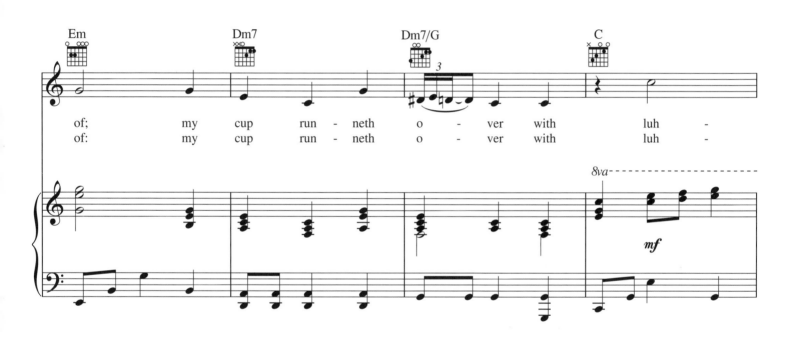

of; my cup run - neth o - ver with luh -
of: my cup run - neth o - ver with luh -

8va

mf

uh - uh - uh - uh -
uh - uh - uh - uh -

MY FUNNY VALENTINE
from BABES IN ARMS

Words by LORENZ HART
Music by RICHARD RODGERS

MY SHIP
from the Musical Production LADY IN THE DARK

Words by IRA GERSHWIN
Music by KURT WEILL

OKLAHOMA
from OKLAHOMA!

Lyrics by OSCAR HAMMERSTEIN II
Music by RICHARD RODGERS

ONCE IN LOVE WITH AMY

from WHERE'S CHARLEY?

By FRANK LOESSER

ONE
from A CHORUS LINE

Music by MARVIN HAMLISCH
Lyric by EDWARD KLEBAN

ONE NIGHT IN BANGKOK

from CHESS

Words and Music by BENNY ANDERSSON,
TIM RICE and BJORN ULVAEUS

Bang-kok! O-ri-en-tal set-ting and the ci-ty don't know what the ci-ty is get-ting, the
Si-am's · gon-na be the wit-ness to the ul-ti-mate test of ce-re-bral fit-ness.

crème de la creme of the chess world in a show with eve-ry-thing but Yul Bryn-ner.
This grips me more than would a mud-dy old riv-er or re-clin-ing Bud-dah.

And thank God I'm on-ly watch-ing the game — con-trol-ling it.

Time flies — does-n't seem a min-ute since the Ti-ro-le-an spa had the chess boys in it.
I don't see you guys rat-ing the kind of mate I'm con-tem-plat-ing. I'd

*Piano top line also vocal top line.

You'll find a god in ev-ery gold-en _____ clois-ter and if you're luck-y then the god's a she. _____ I can feel an an - gel slid-ing up to me.

The American

One town's ve - ry like an - oth - er when your head's down ov- er your pie - ces, broth-er. It's a drag, it's a bore, it's real-ly such a pi - ty to be look-ing at the board, not look-ing at the ci - ty.

THE PARTY'S OVER
from BELLS ARE RINGING

Words by BETTY COMDEN and ADOLPH GREEN
Music by JULE STYNE

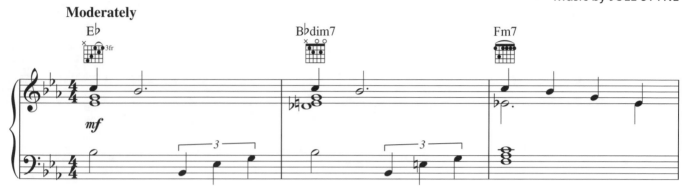

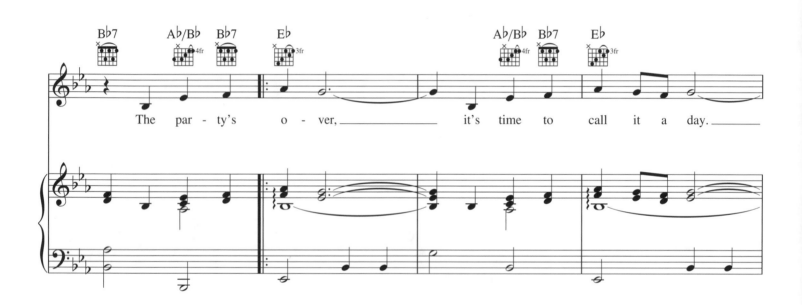

The par-ty's o-ver, _____ it's time to call it a day. _____

_____ They've burst your pret-ty bal-loon and tak-en the moon a-way. _____

SEASONS OF LOVE
from RENT

Words and Music by
JONATHAN LARSON

PROMISES, PROMISES
from PROMISES, PROMISES

Lyric by HAL DAVID
Music by BURT BACHARACH

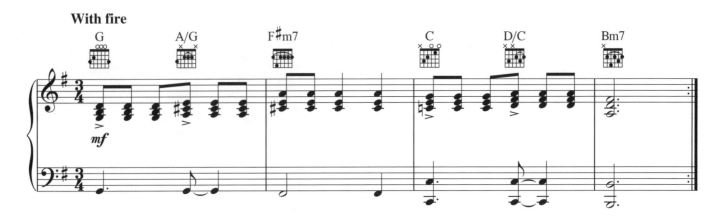

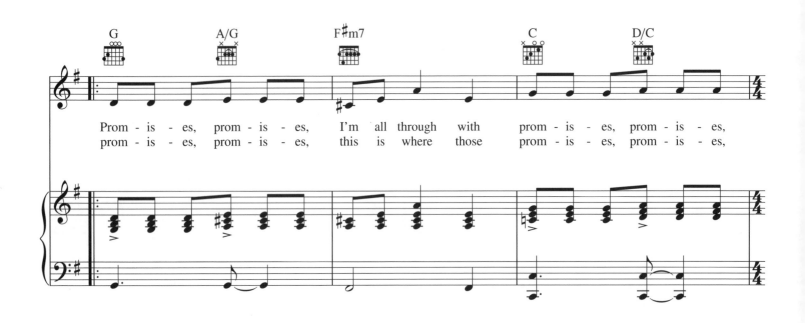

Prom - is - es, prom - is - es, I'm all through with prom - is - es, prom - is - es,
prom - is - es, prom - is - es, this is where those prom - is - es, prom - is - es,

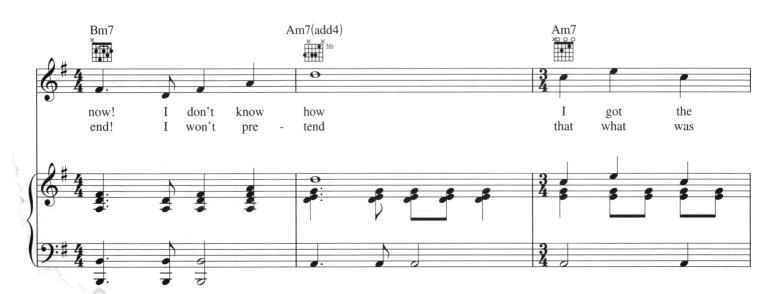

now! I don't know how I got the
end! I won't pre - tend that what the was

SHAKING THE BLUES AWAY
from the Motion Picture Irving Berlin's EASTER PARADE

Words and Music by
IRVING BERLIN

There's an old su-per-sti-tion

SHE'S GOT A WAY

from MOVIN' OUT

Words and Music by
BILLY JOEL

Slow and steady

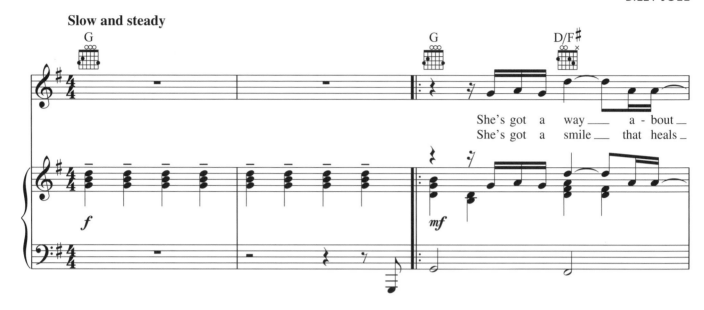

She's got a way ___ a - bout ___
She's got a smile ___ that heals ___

___ her.   I don't know ___ what it is, ___   but I
___ me.   I don't know ___ why it is, ___   but I

know   that I ___   can't   live   with - out ___   her.   She's   got   a   way ___   of
have   to   laugh ___   when   she   re - veals ___   me.   She's   got   a   way ___   of

SHALL WE DANCE?

from THE KING AND I

Lyrics by OSCAR HAMMERSTEIN II
Music by RICHARD RODGERS

Brightly (moderato)

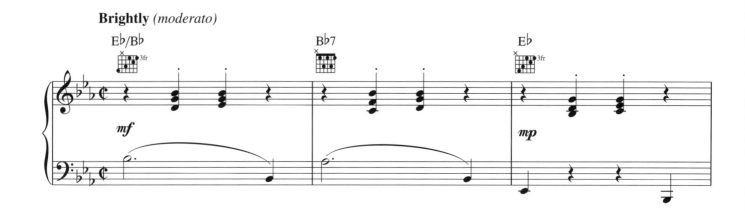

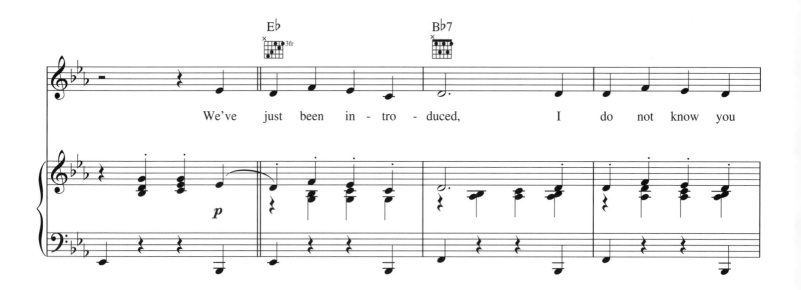

We've just been in-tro-duced, I do not know you

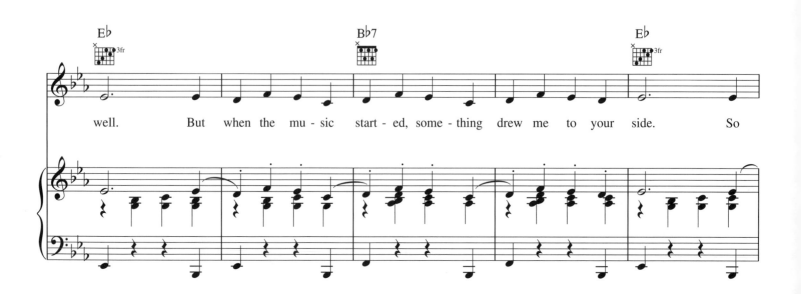

well. But when the mu-sic start-ed, some-thing drew me to your side. So

SMALL WORLD
from GYPSY

Words by STEPHEN SONDHEIM
Music by JULE STYNE

SMOKE GETS IN YOUR EYES

from ROBERTA

Words by OTTO HARBACH
Music by JEROME KERN

SO IN LOVE

from KISS ME, KATE

Words and Music by
COLE PORTER

SOMEBODY LOVES ME
from GEORGE WHITE'S SCANDALS OF 1924

Words by B.G. DeSYLVA and BALLARD MacDONALD
Music by GEORGE GERSHWIN
French Version by EMELIA RENAUD

SOMEONE LIKE YOU

from JEKYLL & HYDE

Words by LESLIE BRICUSSE
Music by FRANK WILDHORN

I peered through win-dows, watched life go by. Dreamed of to-mor-row,
It's like you took my dreams, made each one real. You reached in-side of me

but stayed in-side. The past was hold-ing me,
and made me feel. And now I see a world

THE SONG IS YOU

from MUSIC IN THE AIR

Lyrics by OSCAR HAMMERSTEIN II
Music by JEROME KERN

I hear mu-sic when I look at you, A beau-ti-ful theme of ev-'ry dream I ev-er knew, Down deep in my heart, I hear it play, I feel it

SPEAK LOW

from the Musical Production ONE TOUCH OF VENUS

Words by OGDEN NASH
Music by KURT WEILL

STRANGER IN PARADISE

from KISMET

Words and Music by ROBERT WRIGHT
and GEORGE FORREST
(Music Based on Themes of A. Borodin)

STARLIGHT EXPRESS

from STARLIGHT EXPRESS

Music by ANDREW LLOYD WEBBER
Lyrics by RICHARD STILGOE

Moderately slow

When the night is dark - est, __ o - pen up your mind.

The dream be-gins, _ it's be-com-ing clear - er. __ Lis-ten to the dis - tance, __

SUMMER NIGHTS

from GREASE

Lyric and Music by WARREN CASEY
and JIM JACOBS

TEN CENTS A DANCE
from SIMPLE SIMON

Words by LORENZ HART
Music by RICHARD RODGERS

THEY CALL THE WIND MARIA

from PAINT YOUR WAGON

Words by ALAN JAY LERNER
Music by FREDERICK LOEWE

THANK HEAVEN FOR LITTLE GIRLS

from GIGI

Words by ALAN JAY LERNER
Music by FREDERICK LOEWE

THAT FACE

from THE PRODUCERS

Music and Lyrics by
MEL BROOKS

THERE'S NO BUSINESS LIKE SHOW BUSINESS

from the Stage Production ANNIE GET YOUR GUN

Words and Music by
IRVING BERLIN

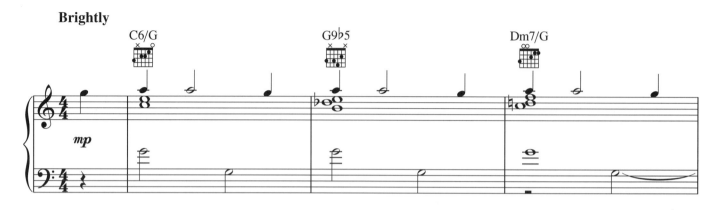

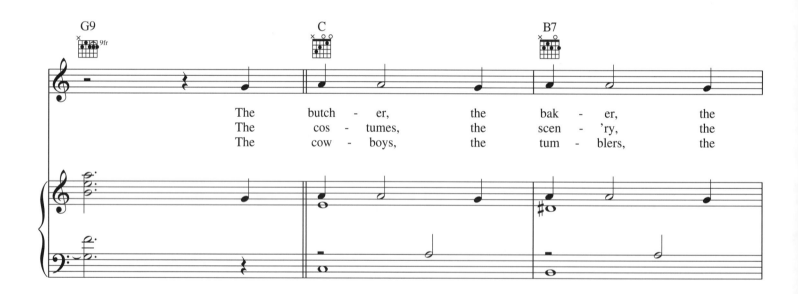

The butch- er, the bak- er, the
The cos- tumes, the scen- 'ry, the
The cow- boys, the tum- blers, the

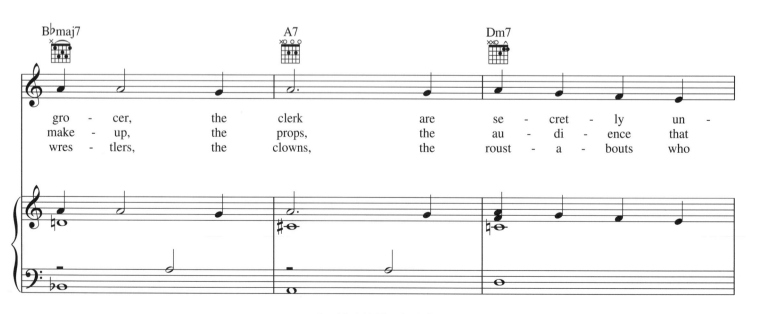

gro- cer, the clerk are se- cret- ly un-
make- up, the props, the au- di- ence that
wres- tlers, the clowns, the roust- a- bouts who

TOMORROW

from the Musical Production ANNIE

Lyric by MARTIN CHARNIN
Music by CHARLES STROUSE

Too Close for Comfort

from the Musical MR. WONDERFUL

Words and Music by JERRY BOCK,
LARRY HOLOFCENER and GEORGE WEISS

The men of science are a bril-liant clan. Just think, just think, they can tell how far it is from

here to a star a-bove. And yet they can-not mea-sure the saf-est dis-tance be-tween

a wo-man and man in love. Since I can-not con-sult a book of

UNEXPECTED SONG
from SONG AND DANCE

Music by ANDREW LLOYD WEBBER
Lyrics by DON BLACK

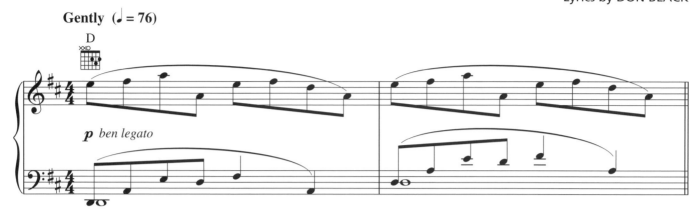

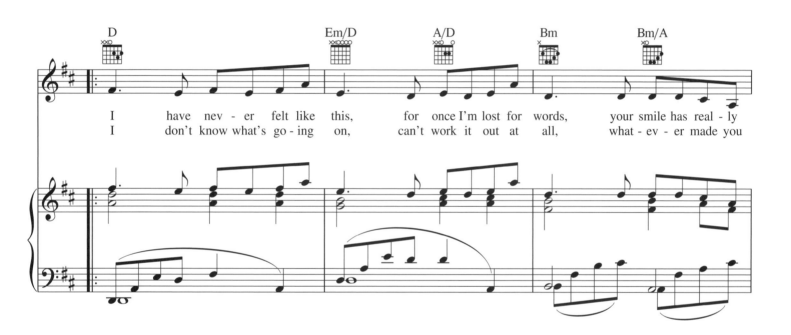

I have nev-er felt like this, for once I'm lost for words, your smile has real-ly
I don't know what's go-ing on, can't work it out at all, what-ev-er made you

thrown me.
choose me?

This is not like me at all, I nev-er thought I'd
I just can't be-lieve my eyes, you look at me as

know — the kind of love you've shown me.
though — you could - n't bear to lose me.

Now, — no mat - ter where I am, no mat - ter what I do, I see your face ap -

pear - ing — like an un - ex - pect - ed song, an un - ex - pect - ed

song that on - ly we are hear - ing. hear - ing.

I have nev - er felt like this, for once I'm lost for

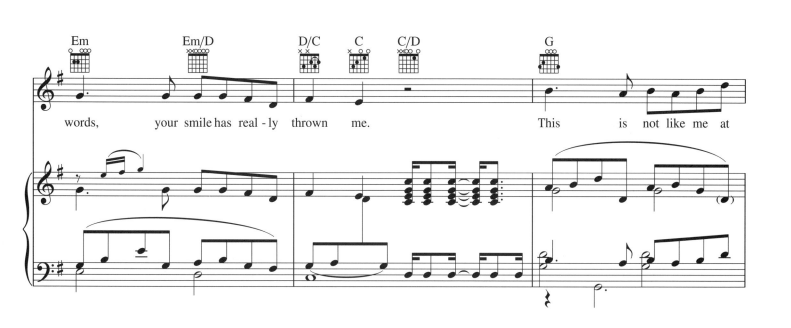

words, your smile has real - ly thrown me. This is not like me at

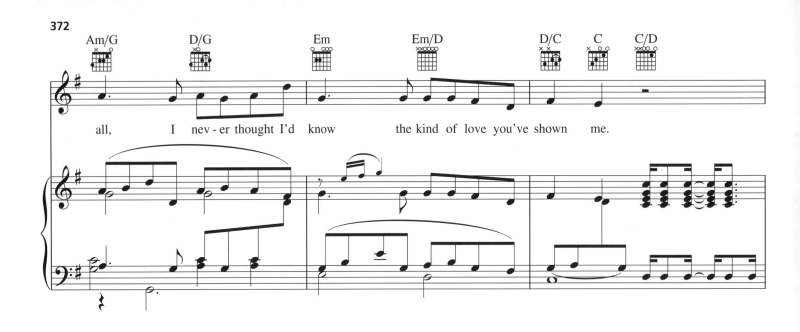

all, I nev-er thought I'd know the kind of love you've shown me.

Now, no mat-ter where I am, no mat-ter what I do, I see your face ap-

pear - ing like an un-ex-pect-ed song, an un-ex-pect-ed

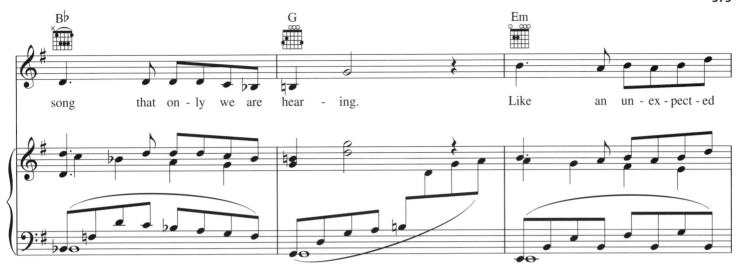

song that on - ly we are hear - ing. Like an un - ex - pect - ed

song, an un - ex - pect - ed song that on - ly we are hear - ing.

WHAT DID I HAVE THAT I DON'T HAVE?

from ON A CLEAR DAY YOU CAN SEE FOREVER

Words by ALAN JAY LERNER
Music by BURTON LANE

WHAT KIND OF FOOL AM I?

from the Musical Production STOP THE WORLD—I WANT TO GET OFF

Words and Music by LESLIE BRICUSSE
and ANTHONY NEWLEY

Moderately slow

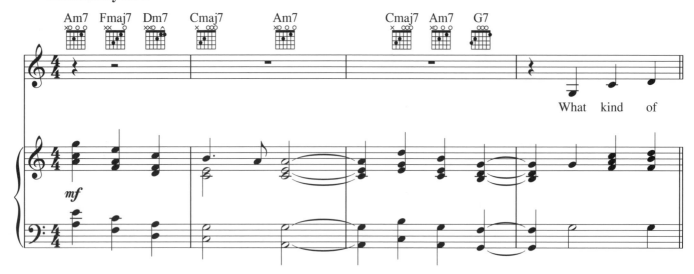

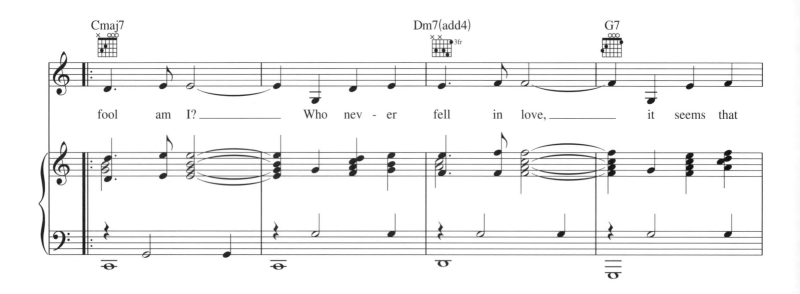

WHERE IS LOVE?

from the Broadway Musical OLIVER!

Words and Music by
LIONEL BART

WHAT'LL I DO?

from MUSIC BOX REVUE OF 1924

Words and Music by
IRVING BERLIN

WHEN WILL SOMEONE HEAR?

from MARTIN GUERRE

Music by CLAUDE-MICHEL SCHÖNBERG
Lyrics by ALAIN BOUBLIL and STEPHEN CLARK

WHY WAS I BORN?

from SWEET ADELINE

Lyrics By OSCAR HAMMERSTEIN II
Music by JEROME KERN

WITH A SONG IN MY HEART

from SPRING IS HERE

Words by LORENZ HART
Music by RICHARD RODGERS

Stacy: Though I know that we meet ev - 'ry night And we
Betty: Oh, the moon's not a moon for a night; And these

could - n't have changed since the last time, To my joy and de - light it's a
stars will not twin - kle and fade out! And the words in my ears will re -

new kind of love at first sight. _____ Though it's you and it's I all the
sound for the rest of my years. _____ In the morn - ing I'll find with de -

WHO CAN I TURN TO
(When Nobody Needs Me)
from THE ROAR OF THE GREASEPAINT – THE SMELL OF THE CROWD

Words and Music by LESLIE BRICUSSE
and ANTHONY NEWLEY

Slowly, with expression

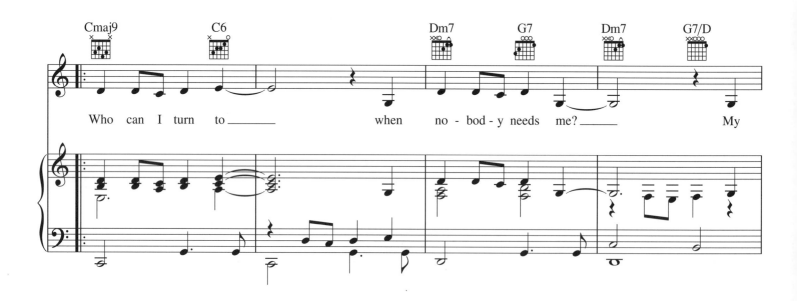

Who can I turn to _____ when no-bod-y needs me? _____ My

heart wants to know and so I must go where des-ti-ny leads me. _____